HOME FROM THE JUNGLE

Anthony Ogbonnaya Chukwu

Title: Home From The Jungle

First Edition: May 2025

Published and Printed By: Wolf Books

Mail address: editorial@wolfboooksindia.com

Website: www.wolfbooksindia.com

ISBN: 978-81-958830-2-8

Edited by: Soma Saha
Cover Design: Wolf Books

Wolf Books
www.wolfbooksindia.com

ABOUT THE BOOK...

The collection . . . offers a glimpse into the emotional journey of the poet. Each poem explores different themes and experiences, from resilience and freedom to heartache and introspection.

The imagery . . . is vivid and evocative, allowing the reader to connect deeply with the emotions conveyed. The poems successfully capture the complexity of human emotions, ranging from pain and sorrow to hope and perseverance.

The language . . . is lyrical, creating a melodic rhythm that adds to the overall beauty of the verses. The use of metaphors and symbolism enhances the depth and meaning of the poems, inviting the reader to reflect on their own experiences and emotions.

While some poems may require multiple readings to fully grasp their intended meaning, they all have a certain rawness and vulnerability that is captivating. The poet's ability to convey personal struggles and triumphs through their words is commendable.

Overall, the collection . . . is thought-provoking and emotive, touching on universal themes of love, loss, and self-discovery. The depth of the poet's emotional journey shines through, making this collection a compelling read for anyone who appreciates introspective and evocative poetry.

~Concetta Pipia

ACKNOWLEDGEMENTS:

The poem "Incredible" appeared in one of the issues published by the Wishbone Words, UK. I thank the group for the permission to reprint.

In particular, I thank my mentor, Professor A. N. Akwanya, a man made by a Soul afraid of blame. Concetta Pipia, whose words are evergreen, has a special place.

For,

My MOTHER, who will retire in 2026 in Igbere.
We look forward to dancing with her at
a light ceremony that will come.

CONTENT

Incredible

COMING ALONG

Redirect me when I am
going toward a hook, lest my peace
is torn

by the sharp side that turns
one into a load of sorrow, which
the adverse forces

delight to see,
to capture, like a probing satellite,
to display to the world that cares for
only what it leans on.

SATISFACTION

The world does not lean on me.

I lean on it, where meteors
of disappointments rain, and disfigure
one to a sorry state.

But how will I regret it when
I know that beams of healing
are constantly in motion in
search of a surface

plane as mine
to derive the utmost satisfaction
as I lie
in its broad companionship?

FROM A SUNLIT SIDE

Nothing else will be
the sun pushing fountains of warmth
as the companionship of the beams
that discovered where it is best to shine

on the plane surface disfigured by rages,
then pushed into the dark, to remain cold
and sleepy.

You will see, from a sunlit side to a full
body bristling with light that gives
the world a new look in its dark situations.

DARK TIMES

Understand that it is the dark
times that define the stars, as they
shine, where eyes send them to
the heart.

But in the brilliance of the day
made by the sun,
we do not see the stars; we do not see
any traces of the stars, even when
we stand where the sun is eclipsed,

where the sun is distanced
from the world, when it is time to
remain close to the admiration
of the human landscape.

DESIRE

I will not pray that no eclipse
should ever occur, since it is clear that the cosmos
cannot expel any of the features of the yin
and the yang bristling with forces.

I will pray to have the strength to come
out, to continue to define myself
in a way that inspires the world.

What will hear me is my core, where energy
is made, and pushed forth to gain
the world that gains it, returning
seascape of beauty to the universe.

CONCERN

Beauty, I pray for this.
And that no deleterious wind
would come again with smoothness
that makes one a bit relaxed and forgetful,
until hard features begin to come from it,
to stain and disfigure where eyes go always.

It is the pictures captured by the
eyes that the heart retains, rousing
its feeling with them.

If I will be asked to explain why life
is the way it is around me,
at least, I will not be bothered about life.
But the heart is full of guesses, and most times,
these become the tools it works with, it
relies on,

armed with great words printed

and sold as definitions and guides.

OTHER BODIES

It is not my wish to rise close to one of
the finest stars in the universe,

since competitive bodies have learned
to send paranoid forces to disfigure
the joy of the one seen, and admired most, even
when they have no intention to occupy
my space when I slip off, and crash,

perhaps raining as meteors where
it is quite strange to be.

All I want is to have my core
bristling with strength, to enable me
rise when I fall, and move when I should,
on my axis running strictly to the reward,

which is warmth.

IN WARMTH

In warmth, my broken parts
will heal,
saving my peace being drilled
up to the surface by rigs of manipulation,
which sacrifice it to its swirling monsters.

I will face seascape
of comfort sending blue beauty to
the heart. What I will have is the strength
of storms expelling unwanted features
of the world to the shores, not
coming under the grips of drought as

streams tolerating the pernicious
forces of the deserts moving as whirlwinds,
as rays,
as dunes, as dust, as flies.

SOME STREAMS IN THE DESERT

In their attempt to bear what
they feel is possible about the desert,

streams, quite peaceful, dried-up thousands
of miles away from the sea,

leaving trails buried with whirlwinds of rage
by the desert. And no one will remember
that life was once sustained at that end
by the victims,

because there are no more signs
to prove that they were once there.

WHAT EYES WILL SEE

If I explode under any narcissistic
disturbances, hot molten ashes will
not be spewed,

to cause fear, to cause death.

I will collapse, a supernova, feeding
rot with strength. What eyes will see is a pulsar
with the smallest beams or no beams
at all,

facing the world that rolls with the sun,
that reverence its rage by building panels
attached to roofs and probing satellites
as proof of its beauty.

What will report,
as facts in sedimentary rocks dug
up with pleasure, that there has been this
victim of abuse?

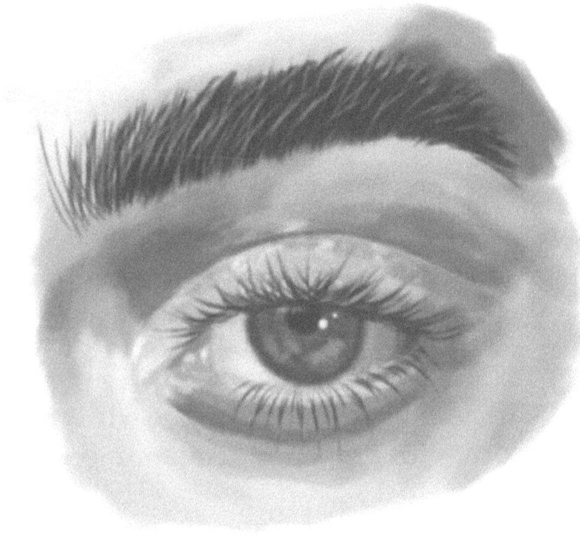

AT THE BEGINNING

I was a victim. The world
could not see me, because
narcissistic abuses spewed droplets of
sulphuric acid into my plain face,

when I thought we were
just beginning to learn to argue with each
other for proper understanding,

because
these deadly forces reside in me after
a smooth encounter.

Now, they explode,
spewing fire, which is not ordinary,
because it is from there that the heavy acids
come up to destroy my face

instead of
the normal smoke that rises from burning
and disappears when whirlwinds are

channeled into the sphere.

LANES

At this point, I will let you
do your things,

because I am tired of striving
to make things work

as if ours is the type of union that people
are begged to get things right,
to do the right thing.

You will be happier
as I believe I will be
on my lane.

RED LOVE

There were no changes. What
fell off was your mask,

which has held me still to your satisfaction.
So, I am not going to waste any time trying
to understand why my place
in your heart suddenly shrank,

releasing all the gravitational love that held
me there, because I am sure
I never had a place in your heart.

You are tired of being who you are not.

And you can't manipulate this reality.
That's why you sit alone in
the sitting room when I

am in need of your arm on the bed.

THE LIGHT

I have seen you as
usual. You are the light,
shining in the open.

I can hear the delighted voices
commenting on it,
assuring a high place for you.
But you are not touching
your own home

even though
there is darkness
and each person is dead to
the other. What are you?

A CERTAIN DIRECTION

It was in that cold heart that
the sea-storm of rage pushed me to have
my knees on the ground,

because I could not flow in its direction,

passing through labyrinths of touch to
God-knows-where. Little did it know I did
not make the rocky vow when I come in contact
with its glistening surface. I have
known oceans, deep, and wide,

and have seen those who did not merit
to drown subdued by their storms,
which still extend fascinating waves
to the world.

STINGS

The story of the past stings
the heart, because it was on the efficient
flow that it went to the broad surface,

where it was thrown on the boulder of rage
that broke it.

Listen! You will hear plaints
the same as pieces of onion boiling in
a small quantity of oil. It may not stop even
when it has been burnt to a cinder by
the situation,

blown into oblivion by the forces
of the corners that once were for it.

ON THE SHORE

I am the one on the shore.

Storms of his heart threw me out
of his blue beauty,
because I could not be subdued, to be buried
with the detritus of lost things held
in his bosom as gifts for me.

But here,
I will find a new day, its sun
composed of warmth that doctors
the body and the soul.

MATTERS ARISING

What could be running on
the mind of a penguin sitting on
the ground after the storm,

its arms stretched by its flanks,
and its tail as a supporter

as its beaks point up
as if they were catching the blowing wind
in the coldness increasing, freezing?

Perhaps it wants the rays of the sun
to make aglow its heart
tainted in the deleterious host,

or it is mocking
whatever thinks it can drown it
suddenly in the crusted matter.

HIS WORLD

His world is not here, because
I watched his steps not different from
those of large dunes on the move,

ending where my world began.

I can't climb it after
stretching neck for the crest, standing
on many tall features, only to see
the same rough sides. His hair, hardy
shrubs,

shaking as if vibrations of nightmares
that he knows are becoming tense
like winds and temperature at the end

of many mountains.

ROUGH FEELING

Rough feelings from the crest
which I was meant to call mine
attacked its victims by piercing talons in their
flesh, dragging to the earthly foot through
the rugged clans of stones on the sides.

I managed to escape, and on false spurs
of complaints are blood, flesh, and bones
of broken victims who, perhaps, had maintained
their stands, looking up to changes on
the narcissistic top.

On this plain is the
true warmth from which this green
peace emerged.

POSSIBILITY

Understand that
it is possible to stand out,
especially when surrounded
by dark circumstances as the stars

whose own darkness is the light from the sun,
that breeds all the terrors
they know. You do not need to shed
your eyes,

to see the sky bristling with beauty—
surprises,
uncountable in
the dark times.

WITH EARTH

When I found this earth, it is
the crust that cuts my feet.

How is this so harsh to cause its spewing
hot molten anger

that wants me to
go down, to lie in rot
forever?

TERRESTRIAL SPIRIT

Terrestrial spirit
tormenting with meteors of abuse,
now slipped off, and shattered,

raining on unknown places. I have not
come to celebrate it, because I am yet
to begin the celebration of my freedom,

healing outside his sphere, where
I glistered in vain. I have come to wonder
why, since he orbited elegantly on
his axis,

taking note of his values,
which were not mine.

WHILE GROPING

I was thinking it was my hands
that went groping for a place to lean on,

but it was my heart,
which has just been wounded by the one
who must have thought it a mongrel

creeping from its hiding. But why was it so?

My words are a breeze at dawn,
and I am not different.
Could it be I am very cool here?

But is it necessary to become an afternoon
—the consumer of strength—or
the dreaded night

for the world, for the season,

for any reason?

HORNS OF DEFIANCE

What saved me were the horns of
defiance grown from the will to remain
what will never go down for the cataclysmic
flow,

although the force dashed me on rocky
situations, breaking many parts.

I am not made for it; I am made for the tree line,
where warmth is the gain, where a bird that
hovers above is an eagle.

And now, I rise,
because it is my shell which was
cracked, not my will.

ABOVE LOW RANGES

Keep me above the low ranges
to hatch a powerful ray at a noted height,

because I like the shock of familiar faces
watching from their galaxies.
I will have no particular description, since
I am not where the rest wish I should be,

yet the bright star remains what it is.

This will move those whose anger will come from
what they will see, which they can't have,
and when they blast under the weight
and heat of anger,

may I not be deformed
by the particles expelled by gravity.

TO HEAVEN

I was waiting.

But it was not you who were coming.
It was storms of flaming heat
as a response to my patience in the open.

It was not you who were coming!

So why should I remain the same
where it is impossible for you
to come, and possible for
me to break down?

WHILE ON A ROCK

Break my heart, panel of
connection,
until I stagger, and beach on a rock.

I will not sink. I will face the sun.
Here, the storms may come again since
it is clear they have
gained the crust of the earth, the sky,
and the deep sea. But the sun too

has gained them except
the strange floor of the sea occupied
by darkness and rot of the earth,

which I do not see as mine now.

STONY, STEEP SIDES

Stony, steep sides
inviting with fair breath from
the tree line

as if I do not know what
it means to

endure what never changes

—narcissistic
forces with extreme temperatures meant
for no human spirit, and being.

THE HEART

From all my torments, I learned

that the heart is
the bare floor of the desert,
and the world the sharp hooves
of the beasts caravanning
so long, so fast, and steadily on it.

It is the sharp edges
that go piercing the skin
of the floor of the desert, especially the part that
has not solidified itself
like a gravel plain touched
by rain and dews all for
the pleasure of the sun
that hardens the surface.

WITH STRENGTH

Fill me with the strength to move on!

I will stand where it is possible to
gain true warmth, because my former place
is a huge dune, unstable, with draining features.

It is impossible to count now the number
of burnt parts I have from it, especially
when I looked forward, and saw its
dominating strength, stretching, strange-shaped,
like devil's mindsets,

with flames of desire above 50ºC.

Other parts of me wilted, except my will—
a kind of testudo—casting the slings of frustration
to the gravel plain, the foundation of
the union. Now, I have made up my mind

to live, and so I move, although painfully,

slowly, looking forward.

AN ADDRESS

I have never taken what life
has given me.

I only flow with the currents of its
river to get to its ocean where I will
explore deeper, and expand to the point
that no waves will ever move me from my place,

unless I move with them in leisure or curious
time, which could be called an adventure

—the true definition of life—that sees some
whales sometimes stranded on the bare shores
of the grave, where hungry natives or beasts
of decomposition

are always ready to do what they are good at
—butchering, breaking into pieces
for their own greater glory.

MOVING

Sand grains hid the rocks in
his heart,
that it is impossible to see any
fascinating feature rising from him.

So, I allowed the whirlwinds from his own
lungs to cover our paths with uncross-
able dunes.

Now, I have turned back,
moving forward, back to the streams,
and back to the tree sides, where
human beings live with
values I can call mine.

AFTER THE WIND

I thought if I leave, whirlwinds
of growth would not only blow away
all the scorching sand grains that made
it impossible for impressive features to
come out from there.

But I have looked back,
what I see are rocks, and remains
of things in the bare heart of "my love"
after the blown of the powerful
winds of change.

INTENSITY

You can't ask me to come back
when something is still burning in your heart,

which I know you are the one
multiplying the intensity of its heat. Fine
endearments in such a case do not prevent
smoke from choking excitements that

move the heart. It is the source of strength
that will lie lifeless. What will enrich our
world, lying, like a savannah at

the beginning of the rain?

MUNA'S LOVE

Muna's love was the full moon
when we were new. But what happened
that I began to see a waning crescent—
Muna sitting on the verandah in the evening
when I am in, or in when I am out,

and preferring to sleep on the cushion
chairs in the other room? There are no words;
there is only the dark face intensifying day by
day, until there is total darkness. I nearly
crashed into a ditch, full of thoughts and hatred
for myself, feeling the heat of madness rising
like the sun to set only when I am no more,

because I cannot tell, because I do
not know what has happened, what just changed
things so dreadfully.

OFFERED SELF

I knew all I had to do was to
offer myself to the atmosphere of love,
reaping fascinations in the same measure
it reaps my light made possible

by the freedom to encounter
the outer sides held by the sun.

But in a situation where what faces you has
more volcanoes sending up droplets of
sulfuric acid that tends to make you invisible
even to yourself, what will you do?

THE FIGURE

Ought I to fix eyes on his red

features, the red features of the loiterer on

the broad bank of the lake, stepping like a chameleon

on the white stones laid by waves?

I called him my soul at the beginning,

and wondered why I should be sitting under

the short roof of the evening restaurant

overlooking the great falls, while he moved

as a breeze from these coconut palms, alone,

hands in trousers pockets. He should be in his

early forties, moving alone, smoothly, just

as a breeze from these coconut palms.

You saw our hands raised, and mine down suddenly,

my face, darkened, back to this roof, this restaurant.

I did not see the man I saw on the bank.

I did not see any human being on the bank.

I did not see.

TAKING OFF

Some who are unstable, slip off,
and crash on those close, leaving
indelible craters or total destruction
like when an egg falls on the ground.

What mends one is nothing! nothing!

And so, the need to move away tormented
me when there was strength enough
to move on, returning
to where it is safe:

this far-off side I could call mine.

PRAYED

I had prayed—and continue to
pray—to be led far away from where
my peace will be a burning sacrifice
for a missile of anger

aiming at the solid foundation to topple,

because I might be burnt to a cinder, to be blown
away by a sudden whirlwind of change.
And the damage may not be left undone,
since it is possible I might be rated
low in releasing enough placatory smoke.
This is my prayer, O my soul made of steel,
you not made of rot.

TRANSFORMED

Slowly, the words that come
to me becomes the hammer, nailing the
peace where it is impossible to tear it
out.

I am the one being transformed
into a lifeless tree in a desert.
Whirlwinds are always sudden here,
and in what way will such a tree

withstand the force that builds massive
dunes from the earth?

THOSE GOING AFAR

Those going far away,
do not let anything delay them;

they do not let anything keep them,
especially when the course
is difficult to take, sharp like solidified
gravel plains, or shimmering as dunes of sand
blown together by horrifying winds,
because in their minds
are the miles, and the time
they expect to cover them.

So, they appear sometimes hurrying as beasts
when you encounter them,
because it appears one definition
rings loud within their hearts:
the world is not the music you dance
with a goblet of wine.

The world is not the ball you attend
holding a lover's hands.
The world is a long route, my dear,
plain here, undulating there, made by
forces we can tell or can't tell.

But meet them when the march is over.
It is the lush faces of
the equatorial landscape that draws
the hives like a magnetic
object with a tremendous
power of attraction.

THE RING

Sometimes, the ring seems

to conflict with the normal movement

round the source of life,

with the heart

always falling on the noted Saturn's

beauty, even though it is clear that many

are successful on their own axis

without any rings.

FROM THE STONY WILL

From the stony will, the knackered
goose escaped the storms, standing
now on the shore where it seems to
be in correspondence with the rays of the sun.

But what images are revolving
round its heart now it is in contact
with warmth, and breeze, stretching its neck
to see
the rest in the sun?

Geese also spread
their wings while basking in the sun,
and it is clear this escaper will not be
found standing with its wet wings
folded. If the joy of its rebirth
will not force it, the cold from the narcissistic
storms,

the force with which they injected
the worst in it will force it to remain a goose it
is in the happiness made by the sun.

AFTER RESURRECTION

What will I miss in a narcissistic
storm that knocked me up and down
after escaping from it?

That it got me
to where I never dreamt in the cold
stony sea, does not mean I was ever in
a place,

because I was never myself.

I will remember the chaotic movements,
and the features that stole life from
me,

and thank whatever made me
a resurrected being today.

TOSSED OUT

Tossed out of the sea, raging waves,
now back to the violent depth, leaving the feet
on the shore which is warmth,

eyes on the four
cardinal points to which the human features,
like a shadow, go, seeking the one who will abide
truly,

who takes the risks involved in dedication.
For this reason, there will be feet at the beauty
of the sea,
wandering leisurely—a couple on the move
on their day of rest.

YOU, WORRIED

Were you worried
that I have reduced my source
of comfort to help an unknown face who
had fallen in the struggle,

knowing full well that the way
is still far, deep, and totally steep?

Who can tell if it was not the waves,
the heat of the day, or his poor calculations,
that knocked him down,

that where he shouldn't end up
almost became his end?

Check if those waves,
heat, and our mistakes are not always going with us.

I see all these in this lifeless way
in which it is possible to encounter similar pains.
It is his accident that made this clear.
So, let's move on!
And leave our peace
right in its scabbard.

OUR WORLD

Together, we built our world–

hearts made of steel—with no crumple
zones to transform us into a bird of long
feet and neck drinking with its whole
head in the colored sea

while standing on a rock on the shore,

because we dream of getting to the end
where we will look back and breathe out deep thanks
—driver and the driven, which I,
the completer (just as peace which
completed me),

am on the road to the grave
that does not scare any part of me now.

OUR HEARTS

You will not see it bound for
where the sun shines harder,

our hearts made of steel, set out for the
warmth trapped by the energy panels from
true dedication, because we have found
the world, and declared it ours, even though

whirlwinds of rage blow up sand, and dirt,
tip them on our bodies, as if
we do not know we are on earth possessed
by rot.

You will see us everywhere like dogs,

satisfied by enormous heat, warmth,
and cold, so that when we fall into the ditch,
whether in this hemisphere or the other,

we will not cry, but sleep.

NEW

New, with the bright soul of
the sky not under the influence of
the evaporating sea,

the sun made this state possible after
driving away the dark waves—sinister
things waiting to pounce, to claw to death.

So, I am the escaped soul, now meant for
the pounding human landscape,

home for me the open-market
place, where we trade noisily, with fearless
measures because of rough boundaries.
But no glistening call will get me
away again,

downward to the waves of

the heart imprisoned by self-obsession.

LIGHTED VOICE

It calls to share its surprises, lightened voice
of importance subdued by
corruption that came upon this sphere,

finding where the red-tongue of fire
tore open to put all where it is better
to huddle like wetted fledglings

in times of dark clouds, heavy prophecies
of lightening, and of the thunder.

Now, it turns cold. But this shouldn't
have been so, because it shows how empty
everywhere is,

where rough steps of giant orders
tear the roof, frightening off the peace
that incubate, and give out, the strength to act.

Ah! There is this shame in saying this,
because
the mind is too heavy to take
and share things now.

TO THE STAR

When you live, and resolve not to
be affected by time, you will live forever

as the soul almost unknown in his own time,

because time honors those who feed
it with nourishing sentiments, which
it defecates into oblivion, and waits for more.

So, star,
you have to be where you are!
Your light will locate the heart when everyone
has settled down. Do not compete,
especially with the sun.

METAMORPHIC

Metamorphic under the great
pleasure of narcissistic control draws
the souls who can't be free after taking
a look,

a touch on the hard-glistening slate
to be worn like a piece of God, because
there is the sun that can't resist this relay,
releasing the beauty to the heart.

So, there
is nothing but warmth and celebration
for the soul heated in the fiery ways of
the magma chamber.

BEING REMAINS

Being remains of the buried
world, sedimentary heart continues to
tear itself under minor pressure

until I put my feet
where it is safe to stand to reap the beauty of
time that age with the speed of light,

leaving the soul to the world.

COMPANION OF A MONSTER

Companion of a monster, are
you the one they believe has hidden
her claws,

waiting to come closer, to unleash the terror
that will pound the heart till it bursts
like a balloon pumped for a ceremony?

It is not because you are bold, in that skin
that makes one look back in admiration.
It is because you think you are kind,
and that there is no other world for you
except that spot.

NEW STAR

New star, not among the ones
falling from light to darkness;
new star, here is the night that keeps
me clear.

The monsters will admire
the light, lifting the fangs to grab
and pull it down; and the mind shall
note it, because it is all possible.

But it is not where it can be possessed

and put in any mind, zip
up, and carried away like ducks in
a storm. Its horns are too long;
its body grown by its own fertilizing will.

MESSAGE

You do not read the messages
in the eyes constructed by the heart,
which eyes can't see.

It is not
because the words are not clear.

You have mastered only spoken
words and meanings in colors
displayed by hands. But this world
is an ocean floor,

and all of us mysteries buried
by detritus of values.

TURNING BACK

The hyena comes with
his laughter when I know it is
waiting to get to my flesh softened
by the desire to love and to be loved.

I turned back, standing now where
it is not safe for it to stand.

It is this human landscape, where
human values are raised like a national
flag on a parade ground.

I am the very soul
out of the crooked reality.

SHAPE, LOST

Shape, lost in the mist of falsehood,

is remembered by the values that created
it, that set it out to get a soft spot.
But it is unfortunate that the narcissistic
blacksmith picked it up with a smile,

went home only to expose it to the furnace
in his heart,

placed on the anvil when
he has no definite shape in his mind.
He beats this part and that part of
the victim until it lies beyond recognition.

It is unfortunate!

VALUE

I am a satellite. Does this mean your
own gravity will ever capture me,

and imprison in your atmosphere
to grace your dramatic being,

terrestrial value, lying
like the fertile earth, which I know?

MORE DARKNESS

The more it is dark here,
the brighter my light. Stars are
excluded from the schemes of things
where it is always bright.

WITH A SPRINKLE OF REALITY

With a sprinkle of reality, you
will quench the part of you saying it
is a grave error to step away from the burning
heart,

because your peace will melt,
and sink into oblivion, leaving a desert
with shape like a devil's mindset. All feet coming
are in a hurry to pass—people not willing
and able to waste their few years on earth
breathing in dust and sand and the fiery
heat that can't be fanned away,

because promising places are not rare,
and those who want them have ears and minds
not frozen by emotion,

not frozen by power and wealth.

ON A DREAM'S BACK

It mounted a dream's back,

soul on its even way to the land that
matters most. What else will follow it,
as it had followed the frightening thunder
shedding strong lights and sounds as if
it had all the answers to the happy end?

It alone comes, the sole witness,
until at the spot where the dream will
come true as life-sustaining seed
germinating on the mound of fulfillment,
the end.

YOUR PATIENCE

Your patience is the rain.

But can it wipe the spots of
the leopard glued to your
atmosphere

like the moon?

PATIENCE FROM FIRE

Patience from fire can't be
melted by the sun

scorching even above 50ºC
to deny some places

a sprinkle of life. What occurs is
the changing of shapes and colors
of the rocks in the ends claimed
by the force.

MOVING

They did not see who they were
looking for. Should they have
occupied the place against the one
looking for you?

They left as
a result, perhaps never to
look back as you who have
yourself or someone else
to host.

FEELING

You will no longer feel you
are on an unknown planet when you
understand where your feet are:
you are on the crust of earth, led by life.

You must have seen some
bottled events, some clearly tagged:
"Don't touch!" with a danger sign
above or below the inscriptions, while life,
the agile teacher,

walks briskly in her hilly shoes,
touching them, even talking while opening
some of their lids, to pour
their nice and horrible contents into other vessels,
changing her countenance in
some cases.

Remember, you are

being led. You know where your feet are.

YOUR HEART

Your heart has been
destroyed—you know this—

and you know you were careful enough,
but life, like a heating afternoon,
hangs above you,

with its feelings all switched off.

What does it know it has melted in
you laying your palm
on your left diaphragm?

CALL ME

Call me when the time is
extremely old, and do not back off
as if the reaping is
all over,

new acts unfolding. Still hold
the number of thoughts that disturb
the heart to enable me lower my
face homeward,

or I remember sadly
the callous moments that could
not pay, and then look back,
perhaps solidifying

as one of the features of
the earth
where a lot of sharable and unshakable

things have happened

since I came.

INTENSITY

Stars of this time, where do I fix
myself in this hive to have
many eyes too all on me?
Because there is
the enormous space, and here is me,

the brightness not merciful like a beast.

Is it that I am stranded now or what?
Why is there no change at all?
Why can't the intensity subside
to enable me swim out

or stand
firm like the rest of the glistening
surfaces, glistening for me?

ENLARGER

He made himself a rat,
the very person you were pursuing
rats with? Don't become the cat!

You know, only few skeletons in labs are real,

but they are what we are looking for, at
least once in our lives,
since we will not scrape away
our skins to know what we should know
about our bones, ourselves.

It is the fake skeletons that dig
us deep, laying the stuff we are made
of, which enlarges our understanding
of our lives.

ANOTHER

I know it is not in my power to
switch on your feelings, but I feel it is
necessary to utter your name aloud,

your height, size, and the way you have gone,
which I can't call mine. If you feel ashamed, if you are
touched, you will come back home; but if your heart
has been stuffed, as it seems, with other
figures (which I have no knowledge of),

you will be there, going, perhaps not turning back.
But there is danger in the solidification
of the mind, and that is the creation of another
being out of a lovely soul. This means
you may not meet the same person you left behind

at the dark times if you ever come back

for any reason.

TO SINK

Pour me away, I will sink
to wake a correlation that bears the happiness,
which great callers can't do without.

Whatever comes under
its shadow is my mind. I have seen them
growing beyond the wind, touching the mind
where hands only wave at, with series of wishes
climbing to get to the top

in this tropical beauty
set by sweeping rays and rains of consistency.
This and more were made to come, but I'm happy
I have seen them happening.

NO ROUTE

There is no route to avoid contact
with the shattered minds, whose
places lie to deflate your spirit filled
with strength. But you can wear
a strong will as if you know you
would be cast down from an aircraft
around the equator,

to have the tear only on the surface,

since further deep lies the engine house,
heart not in plate amour, even as
fragile as it is like an egg. You will
begin well by shielding with steel,
gemstones not for sale or for
the neck, or for any wow.

PHARAOH'S DESIRE I

Is it not funny that Pharaoh
still kept a gun against me after
asking me to leave for refusing to bend,
as if my hands were shaky to pick my
belongings already packed this night?

It could be because I told him boldly
that although I do not know where to
go, the direction to take,
that my heart is made of steel,

which he confirmed
when the unknown gunman he kept
in the kitchen suddenly burst out just
the way Pharaoh answered
questions, as this seemed to be his
response,

because Pharaoh had a satisfied smile
as I knelt under the masked man
until I knocked down the weapon, kicking it in
the dark in the heated
apartment.

I did not expect his screams, loud enough
to seize the attention of a whole commercial city at noon;
his scampering for the door, the neighbors, and the passersby.
I expected the police he called, and
the lie that I brought in a gun,
pointed it at him for asking me to leave his house.

And here, among the cold, dark walls, my voice is
not thunderous as my accuser's, who
even has a witness I know as
the hired assassin, with our neighbors
testifying that they heard
terrible noises that made them think

that terrorists were operating in the apartment.

PHARAOH'S DESIRE II

In the custody, the news stormed,
that Pharaoh and the same Red Sea he
fashioned against me, tore the peace,
as the two struggled against each other's desires.
Mesmerized winds brought the clash and groans
to the camp of torture that his desires kept me.
My jailer called me out of bondage, and said:
'It is true. You did not bring in any gun, and you
never pointed any at him as he lied. You only
kicked it away from the assassin he hired against you
just as you said. The assassin is the
man he called his guest and witness, whom he lied
you also threatened with the gun. It was the duo
that were fighting against each other, because
the one hired to destroy you had gone to
the other to ask for payment. They fought, be-

cause

the hirer said his desire was not achieved, and so

would never pay. Their weapons stripped them naked.

He is a *terrible* villain. I am surprised you still refer

him as your friend. He attempted to destroy you,

don't you know this? Why is he still your friend?

Ah! I am worried!

Why can't humans stay away from where they are not safe?

If you don't know how to do it, they will kill you

and still live.'

FLAMING ARROWS

I told myself that flaming arrows
target the will. If it is inflammable,
what will follow me?

Perhaps thunderous laughter from
the battlements alongside
fingers pointing at the fleeing fool, the writhing
body in the deadly oil

poured from
the top where the boiling had
taken place.

MY WORLD

I lost my world early enough,
and was afraid to find it, because
it erupted fearful things,

even though its foundations are in familiarity
—the things that welcome so dearly,
fertilizing with life. The world I got into
is beautiful, and dry,

because droplets of disappointments
characterized the atmosphere, just as the earthly
features, which remain the same
—most times sadistically scorching.
When it is reasonable to give up, the air
comes close to being temperate.

I get melted, flowing toward
an unknown end.

HOME IN THE JUNGLE

Remember, some days ago,
you told me it was a part of that woman,
who entrusted her store to me, that opened
the door when I was away, and sold eight
bags of her wares. Now, she said you met her
with half of the sales, confessing that
it was you who actually did it, and that I was
aware when it was happening,

when you know I have told her that
it was one of her relatives who got into
her store when I was away just as you told
me when I mentioned that eight bags were
missing. Why are you now shouting, calling
me a traitor, and liar, just for asking you
why you did it, why you made that woman
regret ever trusting me? Is this place

my home? Or am I a forgotten child found and handed to someone in this family?

CALL

I approached, and exchanged

contacts, and clear dreams. But I have called,

to say she should not wait for me,

because I do not hold her flowers,

having been born and brought up on a heap

of thorns! I simply missed the marks of obvious

celebrations seen always all over the weaver birds,

and might be lucky enough to gain

them any day I set eyes on two or more lovers

descending the peak of any tall upland like the Kilimanjaro,

their hands on their waists, minds on nicer

moments to come.

But who will gain the pains

from the familiar passion urging me on?

And what will happen to me if I

continue this way?

FACING UNKNOWN DESTINATION

Why wouldn't I jump down
when you called me to come with all
my skills for whizzing round the source of life,

baring the soft imaginary way which
you can't wait to let me penetrate with you
as we reap warmth,

as we reap strength, and happiness
together on this crust, only to see
your hands on the steering, your mouth closed,

our destination unknown to me,
away from the light I know?

TARGET

Voyager, you on the colorful
lo, is it beauty that calls for
tango,

or volcanic eruptions that spread
horror with fascinations,
targeting the one who does not know what
it means to be superficial?

See it standing out among the rest,

as if it just got the permission
from the highest place to prove its worth
with its active forces that target to gain
the wow of the world even though it
leaves nothing that the world can
lean on,

the colorful lo.

SPECTACLE

Whether the meteors of frustrations
cease or continue to impel
on my heart,

the world will see the glory
of a satellite
with numerous craters,

since the resolve to remain
a charm to the
wheels and soles of the visiting souls
is rooted in my
spirit made of steel.

EVOLVED SOUL

The evolved soul setting out for the fertile spot
has gecko's frictional pad against the slippery
universe stretching to become all I know
in the dark beginning from which I rise
to touch about, to lay hand on the source of strength.

It is clear: strangler fig lays its seeds
on a soft end to get the much-wanted warmth of
the sun at the dark times possessed
again and again by storms of frustrations.

I can't resist the custom. I have refused to
turn back on the difficult days in order not to
slip off from the grace from my will, since I have no
grasping-prehensile tails to stay long
on the top, stretching palms to where fearful

birds perch
and lay their eggs.

I can't rest. It is also
because I need enormous strength
to remain inconspicuous from the eyes of
the opposing forces, the narcissistic predators,

since I will blend in with the green-relative spot
at the end of the struggle.

CHARON

Do you know its mind, Voyager,

you from Charon that seeks no public
validations to be happy, fixing itself
on the farthest cold sky as if it is
well-versed with the law of the jungle
celebrated mostly by schizoid spirits?

I do not know its mind, Charon
fixing itself on the farthest cold
sky as if it is well-versed with the law of
the jungle celebrated mostly by
schizoid spirits.

IN THE CORE

It does not want you, and can't
say it, because you will not be still.

But in its heart is a lake of fire,
which erupts always to keep all dislikes
away.

You know, and see this,
but you are reluctant to examine
the make-up of what is not wanted,
to see if yours are not similar.

All you want is to be there.
Be there, then.

DARK SPOTS

When you see the dark spots,

forget the fascinations emit by the rest
of the body, since those places
could be drowning gullies.

It is an invitation to pull out the radar
for the parts that are a little surprising.

SOURCE

Just a move earned me
stormy peace that buried the craters from
severe narcissistic hits,

leaving smooth heart for its own
circling.

Warmth from its forces
is my strength, which has no waning crescent
as the moon.

WHEN YOU EMERGE

When you emerge, there are
many who won't like to hear the
delighted cries of the world, and time,

let alone see you
bristling with strength, and light,
because they are on courses you
will never call yours.

They are stars,
and if you remove the dark side
of their lives, they are gone.

THE BIRD IN ME

If you perch on a dangling rope,
no matter the wealth of breeze that blows there,
you will not find rest.

You will be tossed up and down
just like a sea duck carried off the shore
by horrifying storms not ready to still,

there on the dangling value far
from the ground, far from
familiarity.

ONE WITH THE DESERT

Understand that one with
the desert will never rest,

because its heart is not fresh
like what you see in
gardens that show fascination—

branches, blossoms, fruits
which a beloved one would
love to hold close to your
nose, your eyes, your arm,
or where you will stand
for what you want—

happiness. You see why anyone
who goes close to the desert
hurries to leave?

Many have suggested that it is
because of the basilisk's breath
of the sun, and winds
that it dotes on.

There is simply no flesh in bones.
And even dogs do not go
for barren bones,
which are what deserts are.

MY STRENGTH

My strength is just a vulture's egg.
If it hatches as my heart desires,
it is my chick—a part of me. But if it dies,
it is my food. Eating it gives me what I need to be
who I am:

a soul incapable of sinking in despair despite
the mountains of rocky circumstances breaking
the soul that hits itself on them unknowingly.

That's why you have known me today.

I prepared always for the things
that should make me die in sorrow.

STRENGTH

In trying to run away from continual despair,

I have even enrolled myself into the priesthood of eternity—

the supposed order of Melchizedek of Salem and of old.

Ambivalence urged me on there

where I was obliged to get it right by willfulness

so profound (you won't believe it!) at the front where it

read out daily the vow I must make to be successfully

removed from the humanity I was to serve:

I will please the maker of all things;

I will please nothing else, even myself.

'But you must go mildly with the wild eye

of the bird upon this bell-ruled servanthood

until you pass all the ancient tests

on this Magellan journey into the holy halo'

was the resolution in my submerged spirit

where nothing else was to follow me

or else—we were warned on the orientation day

—

we would all burn to a cinder by the enormous

pressure from the bosom of Mercy

that sustains the world (according to the astral stars gone

or firmly sitting where we bowed and took order).

The soft canticle said it all: *sic transit gloria mundi.*

THE LEAFLESS SPIRIT

The wind shakes the slim trunk

of the leafless spirit,
baring most of its puissance
slightly deepen in the sands,

but it is still alive;

although bent so low that almost all parts of
it touches the terrifying sand,

it is still alive,

tough spirit
facing the sun sitting fully
like a supreme authority,
with no leaves, or many roots
running deep.

We found it standing,

and alive.

IN A STRANGE TIME LIKE THIS

All of us
in a strange time like this
can tell where we have started our journeys;

but how it is going to end,
the rewards to associate with it—
this—oh this is surely in the surfuric clouds!

Because what we know are
the rough courses, the echoes
of the waves, the moments of
insurgent heat—all of these that
do not know us—even when
the world gives us the dates
and the streams of reassurances.

So, the overwhelmed hearts listen,

but do not hear convincingly
that the difficulties are just going to end soon—
the rough courses, the echoes
of the waves, the moment of
the insurgent heat.

And while thinking that the oddities
remain forever with them,
their spirits go down
like a massive ship
in a deadly contact with a massive
rock from the depth of the sea.

You are gone, finest or not,
drowned to land
in detritus forever.

LARGE BODIES

Larger bodies, moved by the
urge to discover who they really
are, sometimes throw themselves
on others. If you are the victim, and you
smash, and rain as meteors of sorrow
on the hearts that bear you as a priority,
they whizz on, and perhaps no

noise will be heard, but if they are
the ones who smash on you,
as it sometimes happens, you are
the devil, red, full of horns, since their
broken parts will rain so wide (as enormous
bodies they are) that almost everything is
touched. You will see that this heaven
made by the pioneers is
not your home. The woman holding

the sword and the scale will lead you away.

She is mute, and she is blind.
You should know what it means to
be both mute and blind in this
chaotic entity called the universe.

FOR A PERFECT DANCER

Finding a perfect dancer

who continues even when there
is no music is the dream composed
of gains that swoon the heart

in the paradise where there is no grave,
where there is a fruit you cannot eat
which lies in your own chord.

ABOUT THE SUN

The sun you see is utterly rich, yet
it does not care about the places of
the numerous stars.

And so, it hits the universe
hard, and no darkness is found. How
can you then find the stars?

You find the sun, and you find it always,
of course, because some of its worth
comes stretching here and there,
touching this and that, and you
can't deny it.

It becomes the topic;
it becomes the life.
But it is the darkness to the stars.
Who is there to bother

themselves about this occurrence?

MARK, AND TIME

It is possible to prosper in this desert,

because the amount of energy erupting
both fearful and fascinating things show
that the best is yet to come. Only those
who are lively, who are daring like the wind, will live,

of course, above the rot of the crusted polity

upon which the finest, the wisest have trodden,
some,
saved by the ways they
devised with their minds, crossed the miles,
the gravel plains with no human features,

getting to the human landscape with motivations,
while some forgotten because of

the weakness of their beasts, and their souls,

that they could not touch the mark of

recognition and longevity.

YOU

You are a star;
you are nothing else.

Do not be carried away by the
veiling darkness created by the sun
who sit imposingly close to the world.

Night is your light. At the time,
the soul is at rest,
you will be seen, given your
place in the heart, moon or no moon,

you will shine on the sky
at the dark time.

ASTRIDE

I prefer to have a foot broken.

That's why I am the colossus
standing astride
the life we live together.

And having life flowing below,
I feel all its cooling essences.

THE WORD

For my mother...

I

You once dropped a magazine
about our modern pioneers, published
in 1990,

when I was born. You said: "See,
if you will do what those great men and women
did, Igbere Welfare Union, who printed this,
will write your name where they have written
those of the pioneers."

What did the pioneers do? They trekked
miles to get sharpened, and here is the school
they brought around 1916, which made
everyone believed they are the sun,

the center of our universe. What else is to be
done?

There is no trekking these days;
there are no more leopards stealing into
Bush Schools, or jaguars, and headhunters on
the long forest paths to school.
Even bicycles, such as the one a pioneer
displayed proudly
in one of the photos, are archaic to
use for pleasure today,
although they worked very hard to buy
them for satisfaction as they labored on them
on the rough roads to distances. For these reasons,
I will become the word that will talk about
the light of the sun, since all of us are planets
circulating it.

The magazine is my orbit.

II

You remember that day you

transformed me into a humanless landscape
by uttering the terror: *You know you will be doing a lot*
of thinking when you take up the pen? You know?
What I mean is the exploration of the inner world.

Your eyes were on the shelves of
the voluminous anthologies, which you
said were supplied to father by the same group who
equipped the huge library at the University of Nigeria.
According to you, such a career as writing
would really deny
me true happiness, since I would be exploring
and uttering those
things that should be left alone,

which would bring either
wild romanticism about life, or stupid skepticism
that enraptures
consciousness like hard drugs.

Your eyes were on my mind
as if your powerful rays would melt

whatever was in there telling me to write,
which you said was just the same
as creating another being
out of what one has always been.

Your hands were on the huge shelves behind
us as if it was where all the woes in heaven and earth
were imprisoned with pen, perhaps waiting
for me to try coming deeper as a pen,
and your praying posture said it all: you were
interested in breaking anything charming
about exploring the inner world wrapped in words.

That was why I took that glass of water,
and offered you to drink
to see if you could doze off on
the large cushion chair. And it seemed to
confirm your fears, because you held
the water which you did not ask for,
and were looking at me, mute, with
eyes opened so wide
that one would think

you were rehearsing a chant, a ritual.

You were whirlwinding your tears together
to rain it without any harsh lightening
or thunder, because you actually poured the water
yourself in that glass kept before us. It was one
of the reasons why I took an anthology behind
you, and went back, not feeling strange at all.
I could not be watching you fanning yourself with
a lighter magazine
despite the enormous Ox fan almost
blowing up your gown.

THE WALL

In memory of my father

I

I remember. My father,

who worshipped only in Cathedrals on

very special seasons, knew the reflecting high walls,

which he called his children. Meaning I am one of

those walls, reflecting. Whatever this means,

I understood he enjoyed wider circles,

and was found at home while occupying a whole pew,

sometimes with my mother, and my grown siblings, at the front.

I sat behind them, reflecting on the altar messages, while his

eyes went from wall to wall, to the heavenly ceiling possessed by echoes, wild birds, and artworks. What message was

written on them? He said, "Tomorrow." What on earth

meant tomorrow? He said, "The reflection time. And believe me,

if you will, there will be nothing else. You will be reflected on

as you reflect and even apply in your life what is said here

by the altar. That's it. And that's all. If you don't get it, it is not my fault."

What is there to argue about with my father, even though

he pushed to argue with his whole being in order

to laugh out loud when you get angry or point out a derogatory

word in his responses. Or he frowned when

you turned happy in the argument perhaps

as a result of his blunders (grammar, and sense), my father

who did not think people did make out laughter

and anger. I grew up bearing the images of the shining walls,

telling myself always: you must reflect like
the walls but not to humor your father who
said you were one of them.

II

In what way was I reflecting,

that a priest should tap my back in Enugu, and asked:

"What on earth is Ernest Hemingway talking about

in his *The Old Man and the Sea?* You see,

he says sea, he says harpoon, he says net, he says

birds, he says the sun, he says distant colleagues of

the old wretched man facing the wild winds and the boats,

and the good boy, and the newspaper about football,

and his inability to pray always, and deep. What else?"

I said to him: No need to ask, Father.

You know we are all wretched in different ways, getting older

alarmingly on this strange sea, which is earth?

If you listen well, you will

hear other fishermen so much like furious weather,

howling, and sailing across on their boats

as if they were teenage boys in Guinea sailing

away from sight for circumcision,

armed with sharpened dreams

of making a big living that attracts attention.

Even if concerning storms should come

bringing some unfortunate forces

from the hadal zone perhaps targeting

to eat up the gain you are dragging to the shore,

be sure you may not be lucky enough to

find kind faces turning to just take a look.

What else happened to Ernest Hemingway's Old Man in

the storms of rewards?

IN THE DUNGEON

I know you are the one who will
call me out of this dungeon.
That is why I could not wait.

I have been sitting in the crowd, but I
was alone despite the currents of
hope tossing me from edge to edge.
Just look at me from that top.

Your rays will do the miracle—parting
the troubled night for a great walk
to where there are stones to stand
against the sinking policies of
the clouded time

broken, sold to the

corrupt storms, and the darkness targeting

my soul to eclipse forever.

INCREDIBLE

It is incredible
that I have not perished
in the heat of this tough time,
which bares the space for
the pleasure of the least—

trauma—invisible,
lurking in the air
like a beast of wings and claws,
where the scampering world
goes dropping and rolling
from shocks to shocks—
this moment when the means
of survival is too thin
to lift one up for the cause,

and the land sinks here,
and bares what looks like caltrops

that pierce the hooves of hope,
orderliness, and service,
from the hardened plains very
unknown to rainfalls and dews,
to the top where the whirlwinds
struggle like demons seeking
limelight.
Desert!
I do not know! I cannot tell!
what sustains me here
where it is easy to fall as a result
of the swirling forces on
the hardscrabble way
where it is hard to rise,
to see, to reach out to the world,
where it is hard to rise, to move,
to move on! and on!

But having deepens my heart
in the fertile events,
with spirit made of steel,

I know I will never fall
even if the skins of my hope are torn
and all its contents poured out
in the wild designation.

www.ingramcontent.com/pod-product-compliance
Ingram Content Group UK Ltd.
Pitfield, Milton Keynes, MK11 3LW, UK
UKHW041346190726
13845UKWH00026B/455

9 788195 883028